I0465127

ANIMALS
Being Wild
Coloring Book

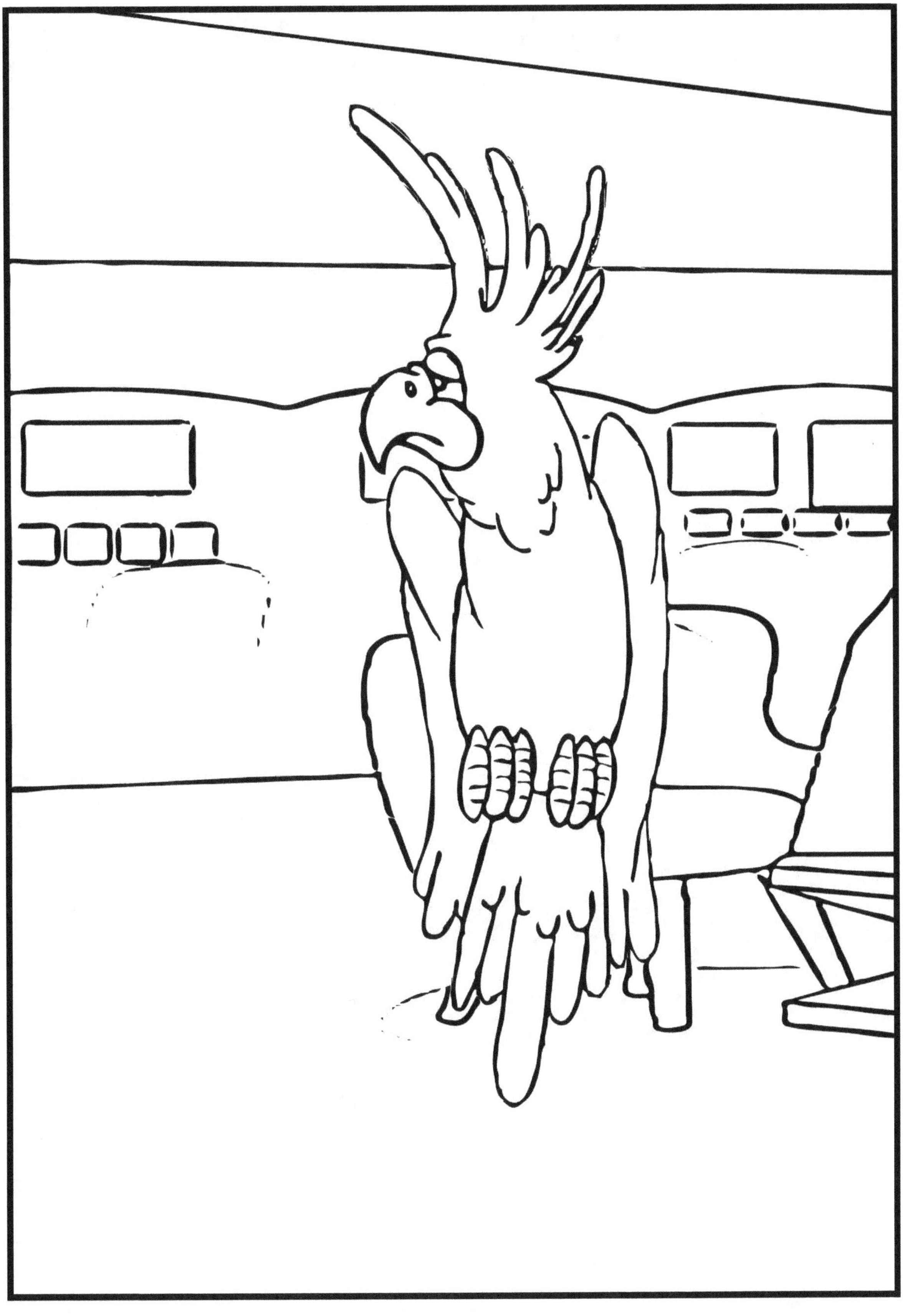

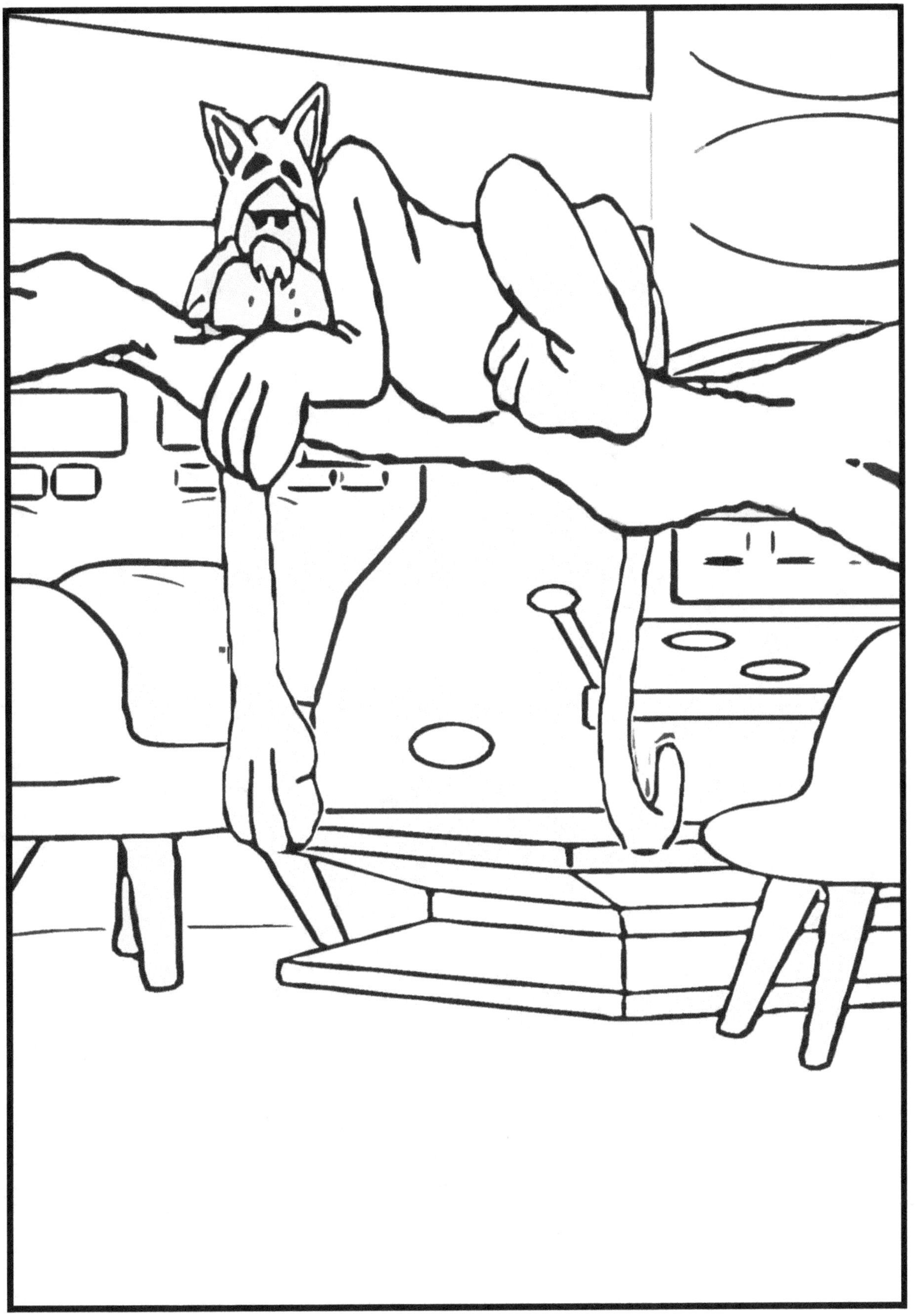

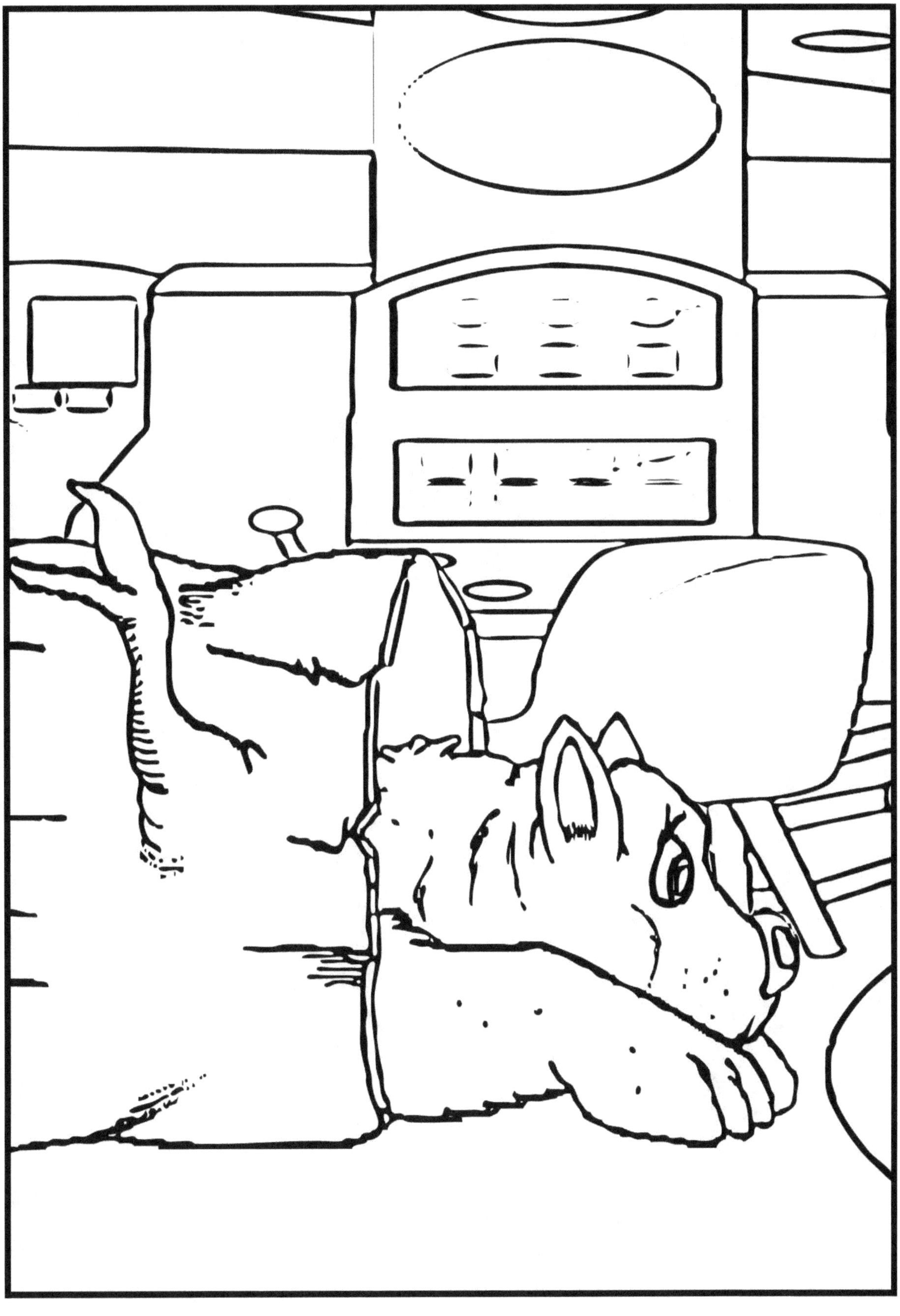

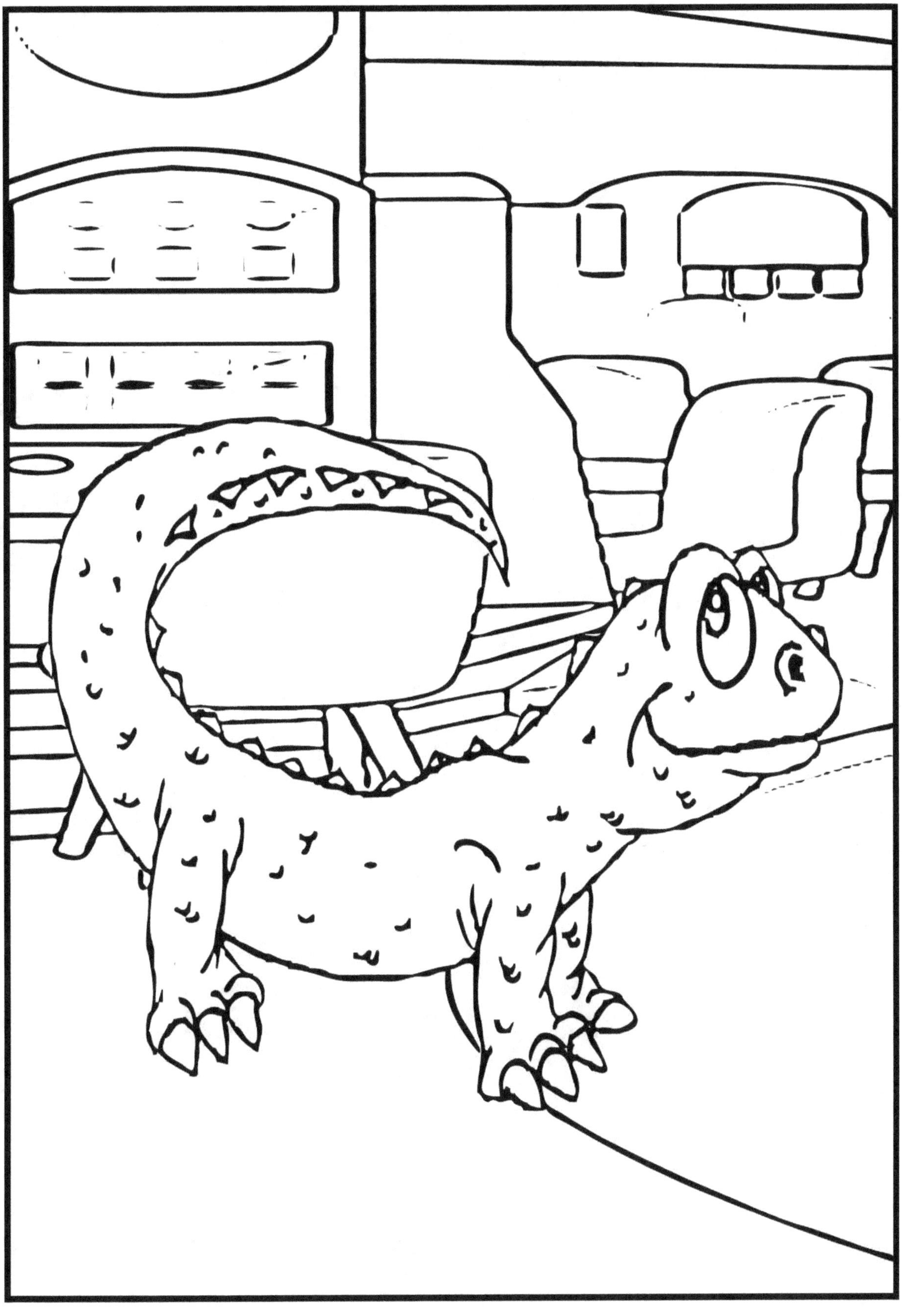

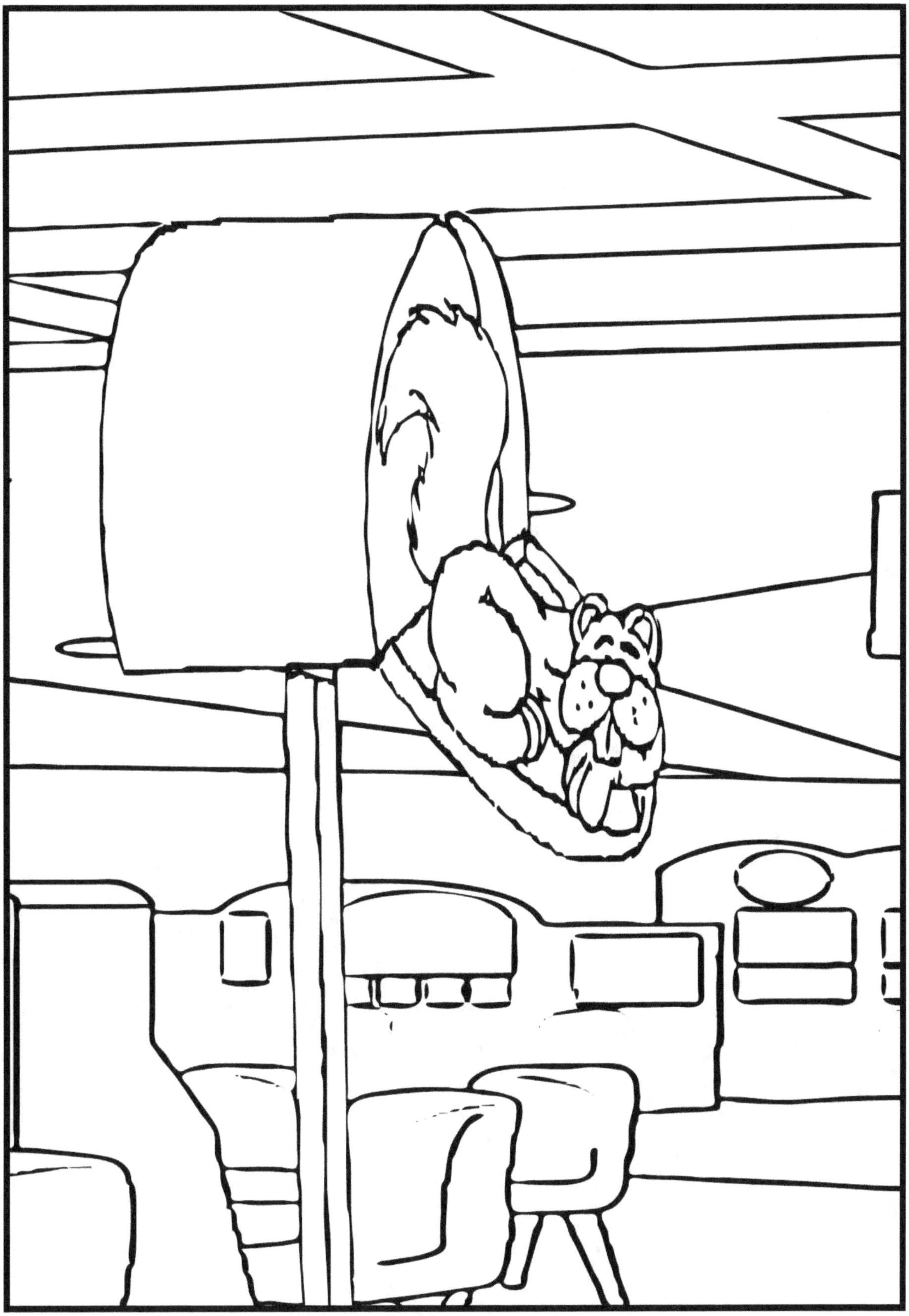

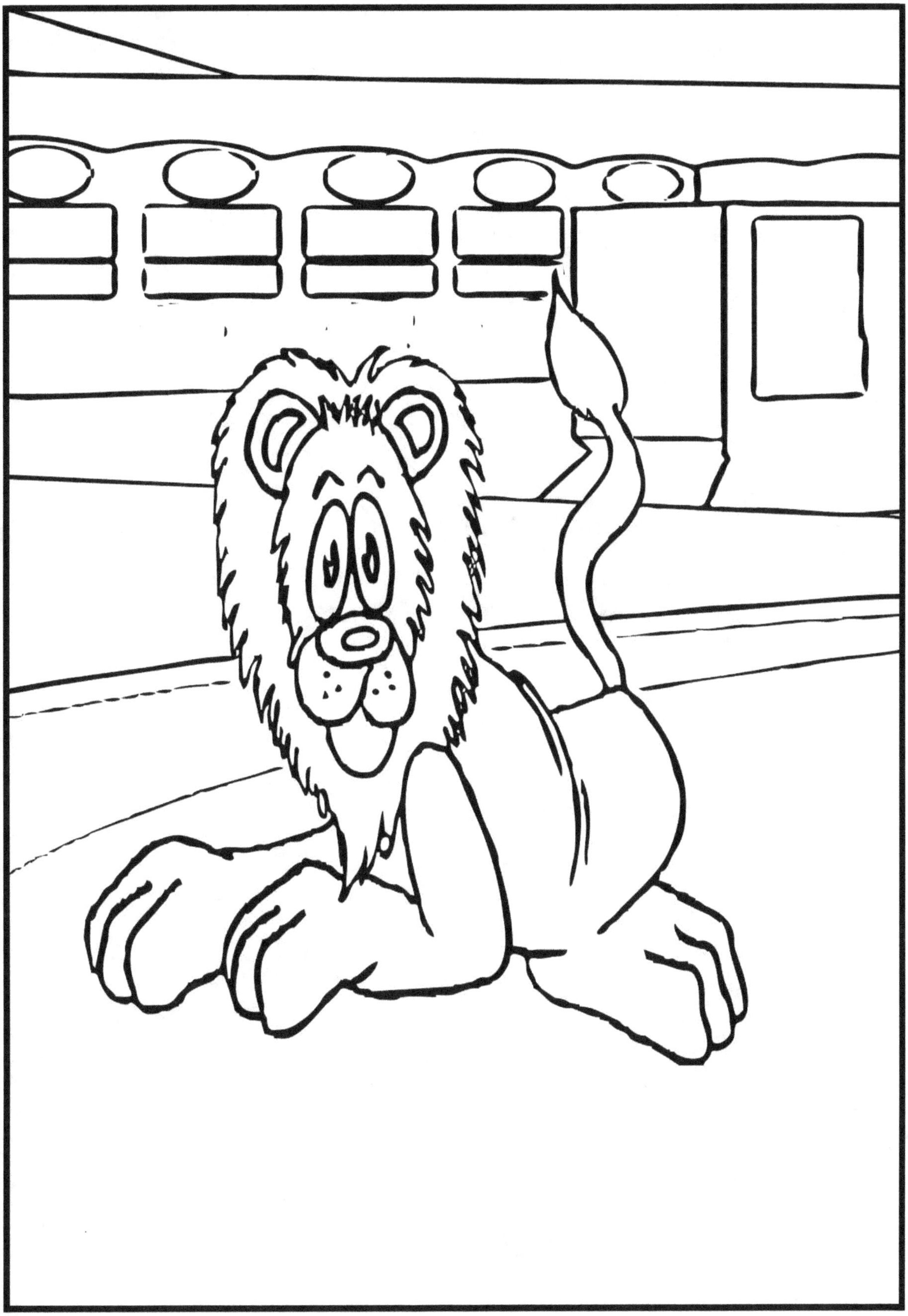

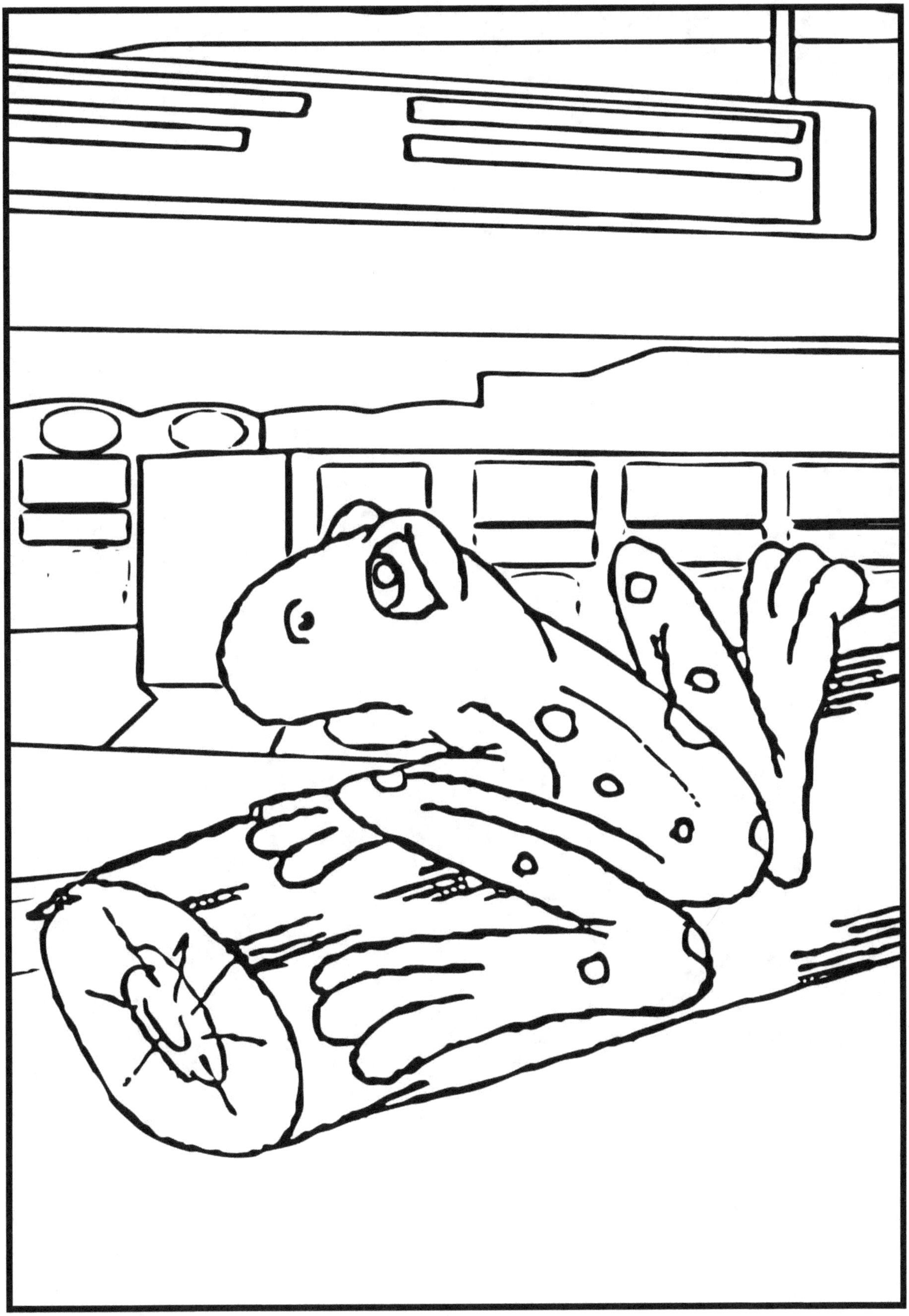

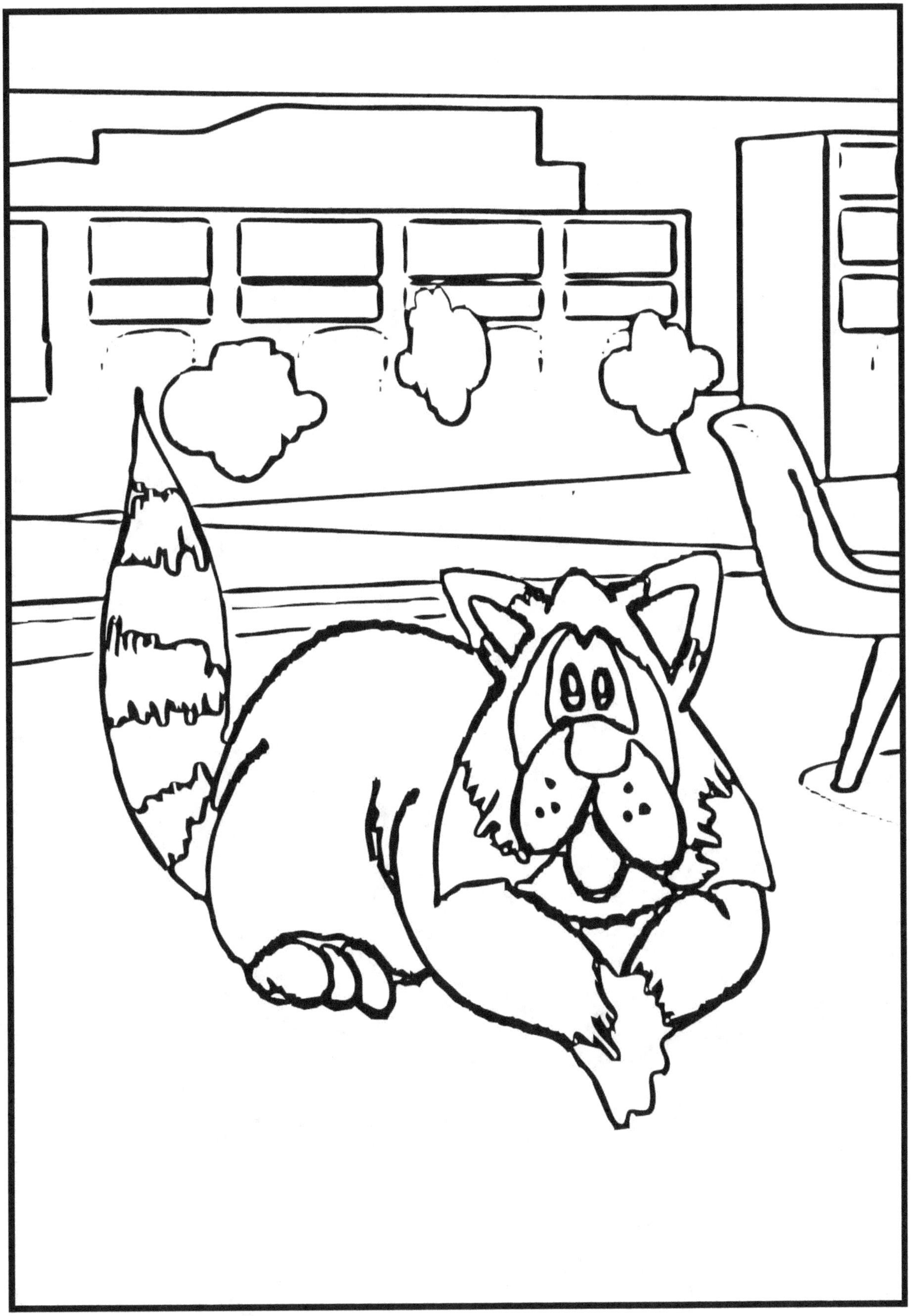

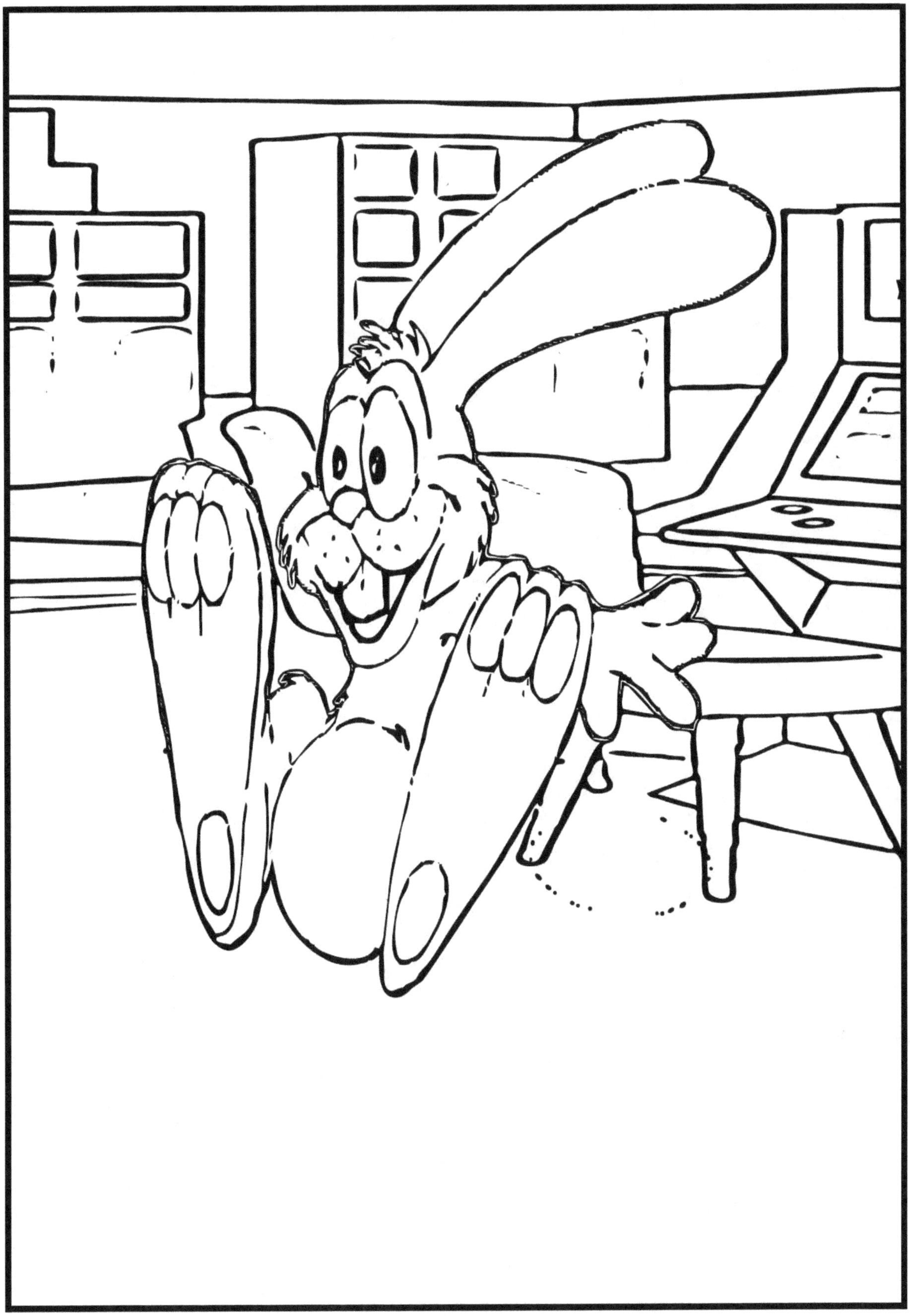

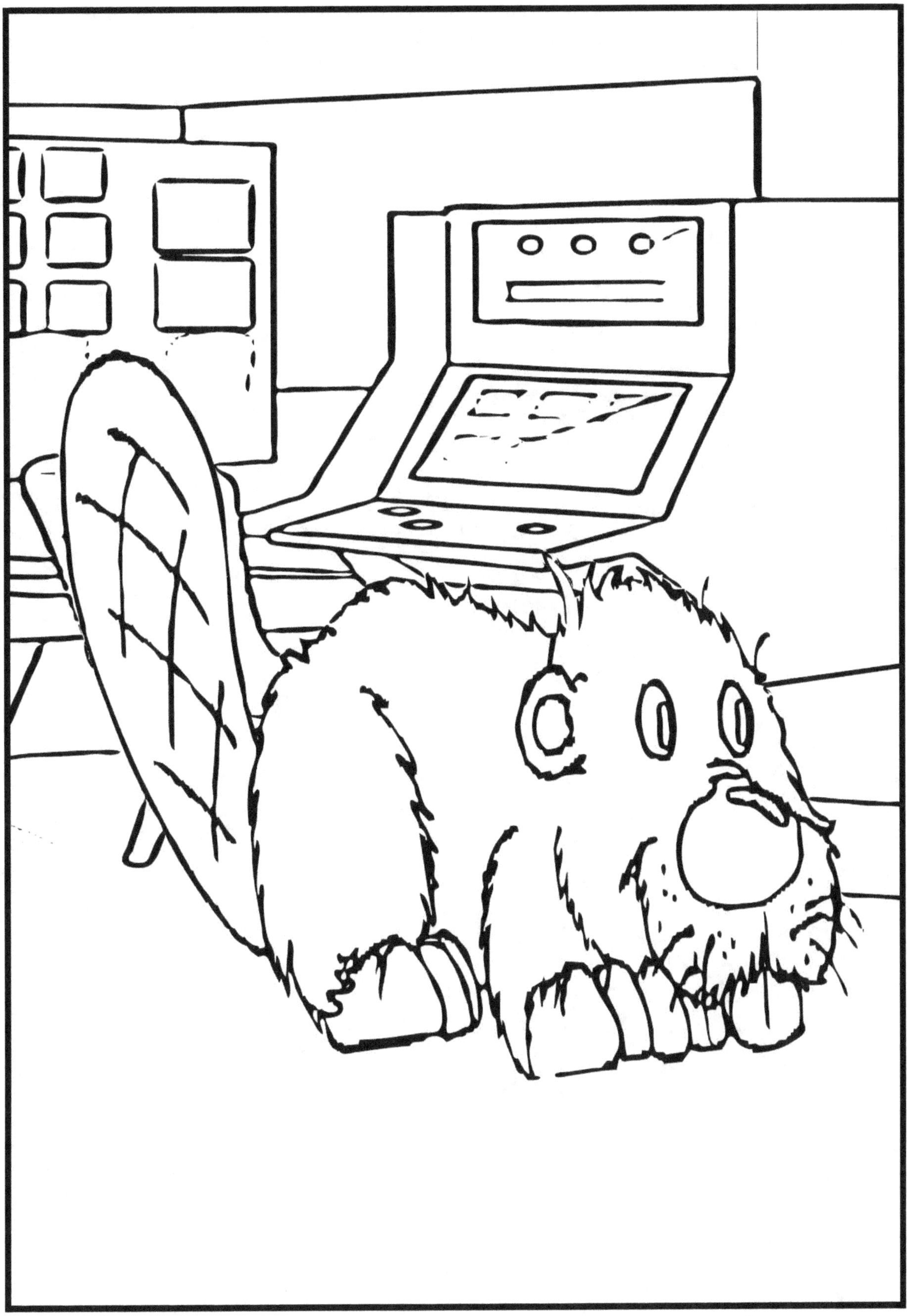

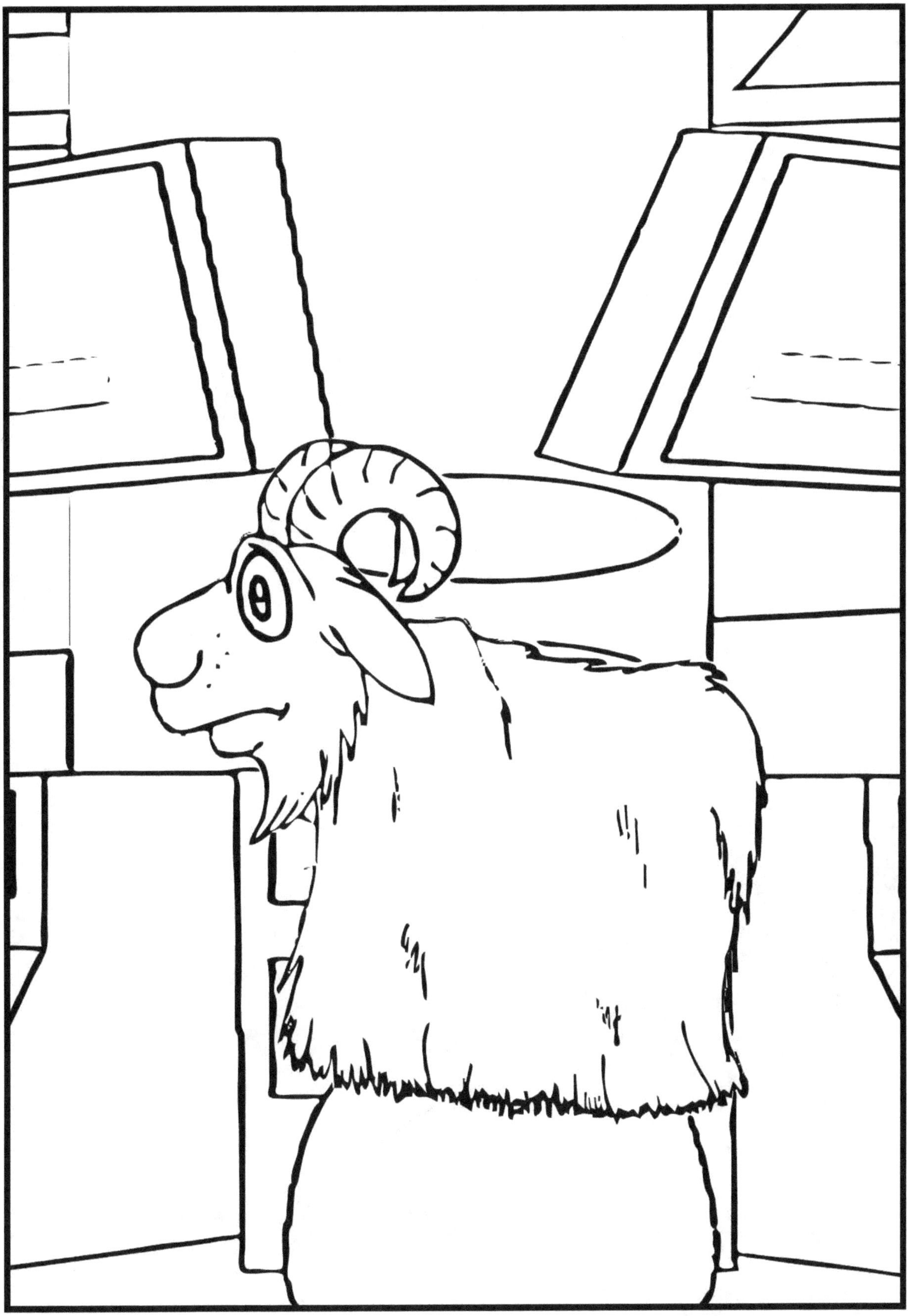

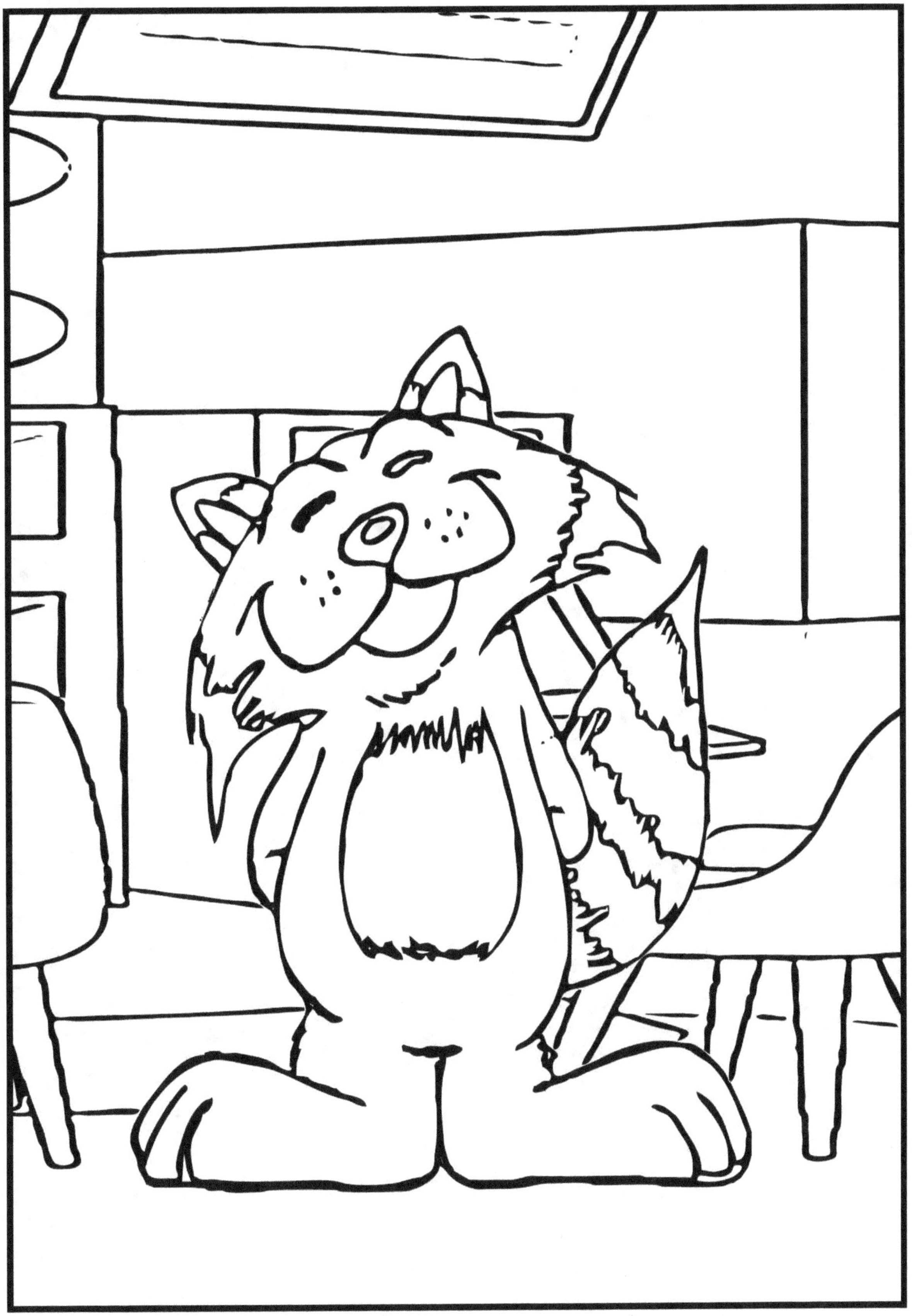

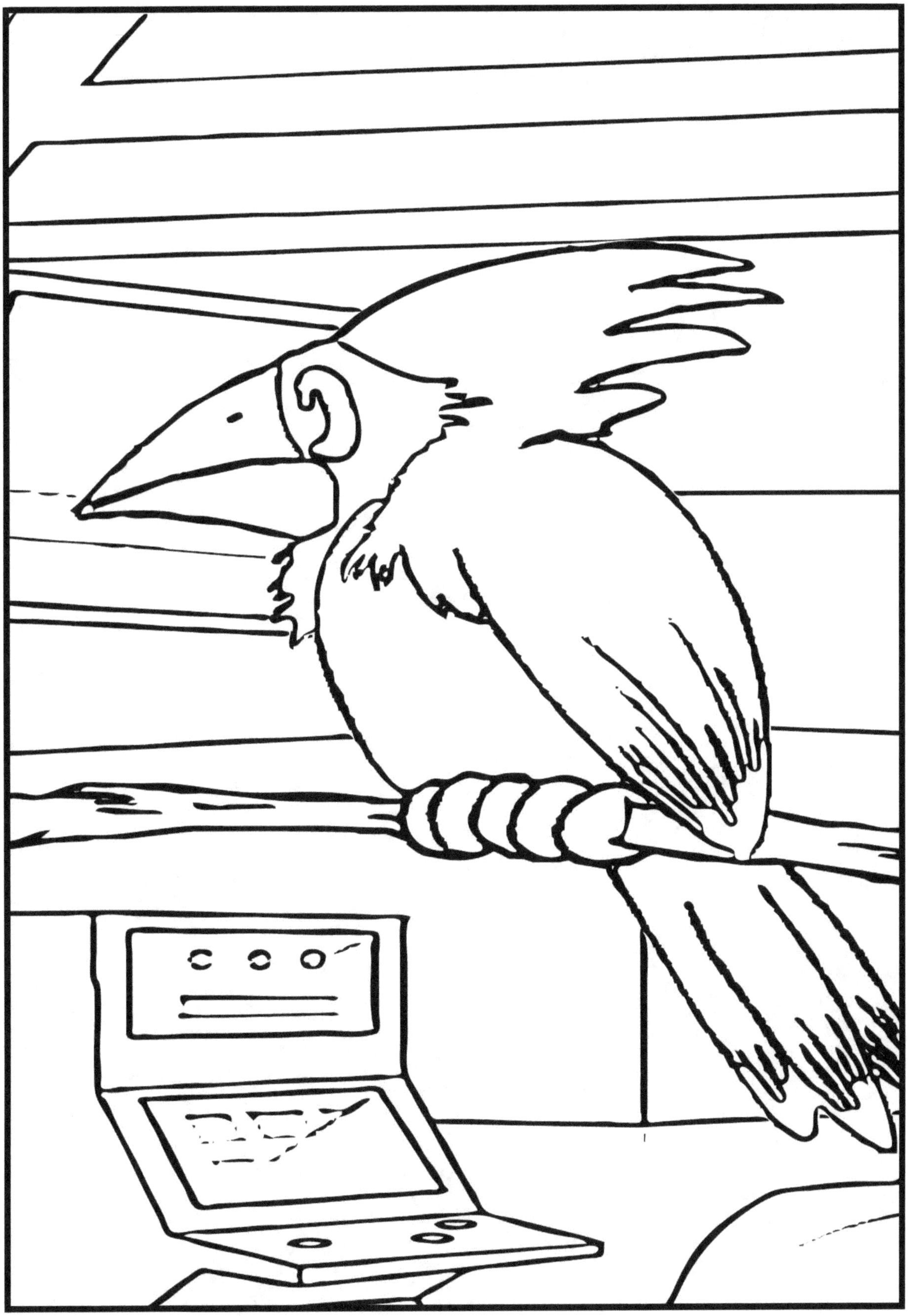

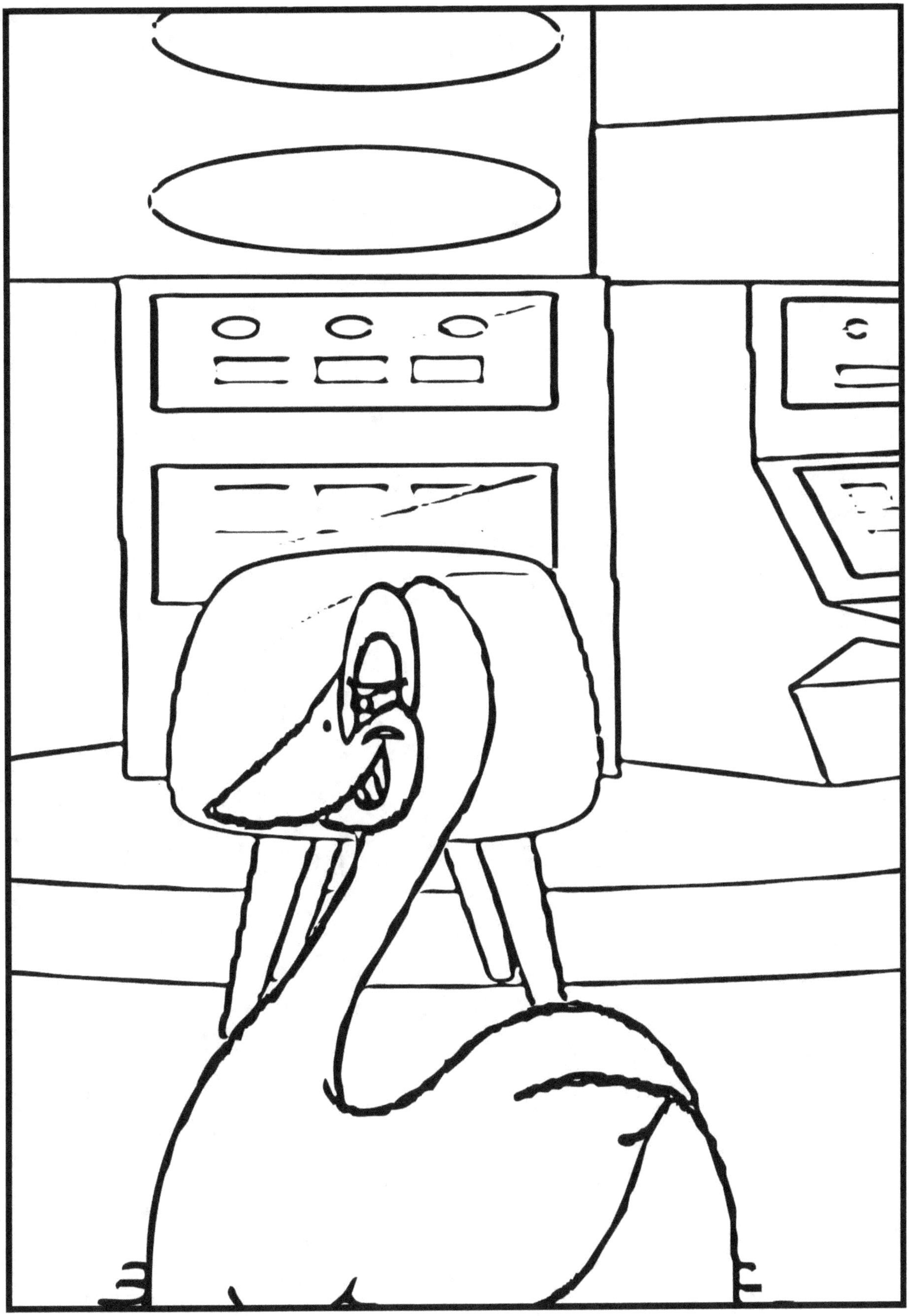

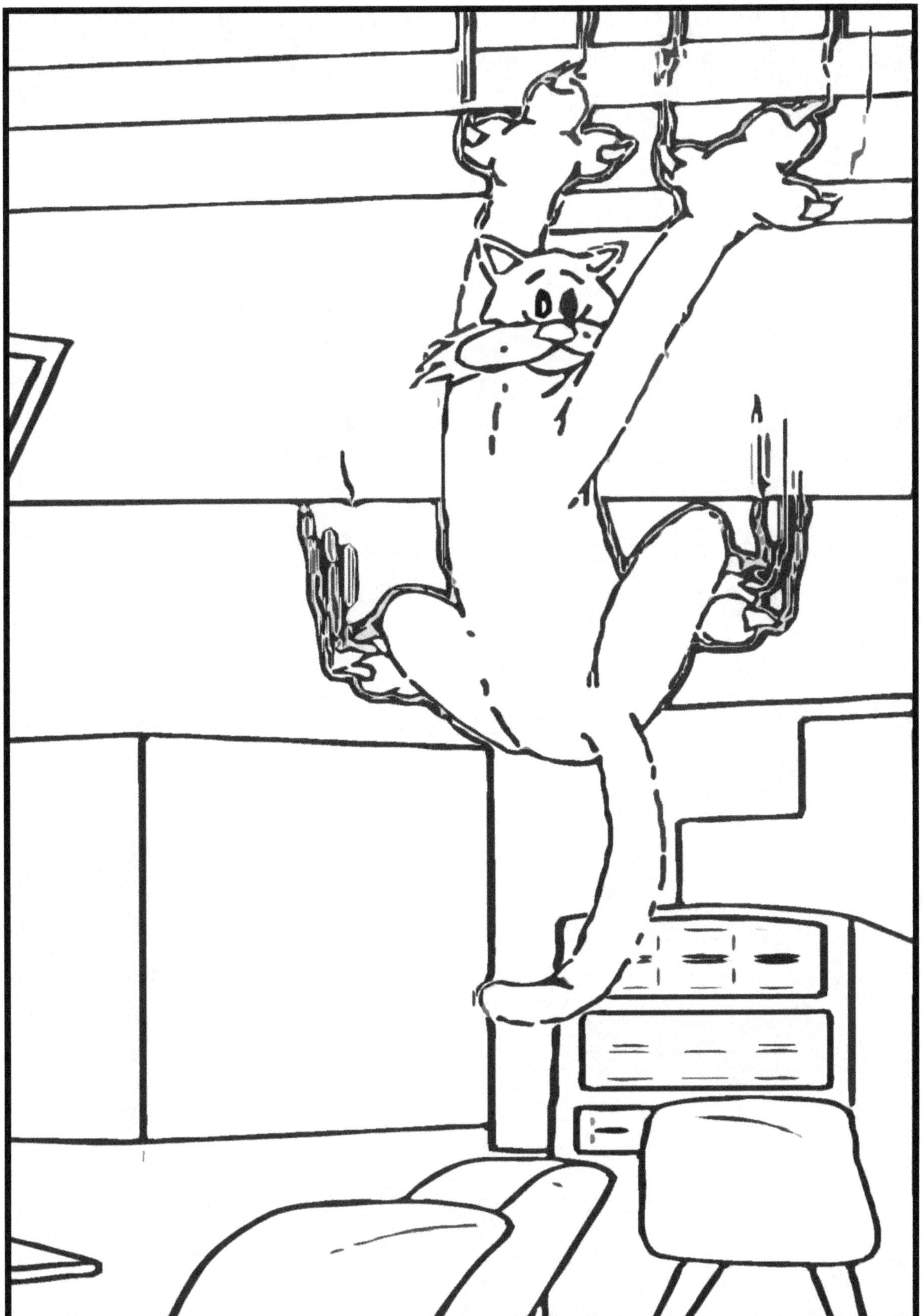

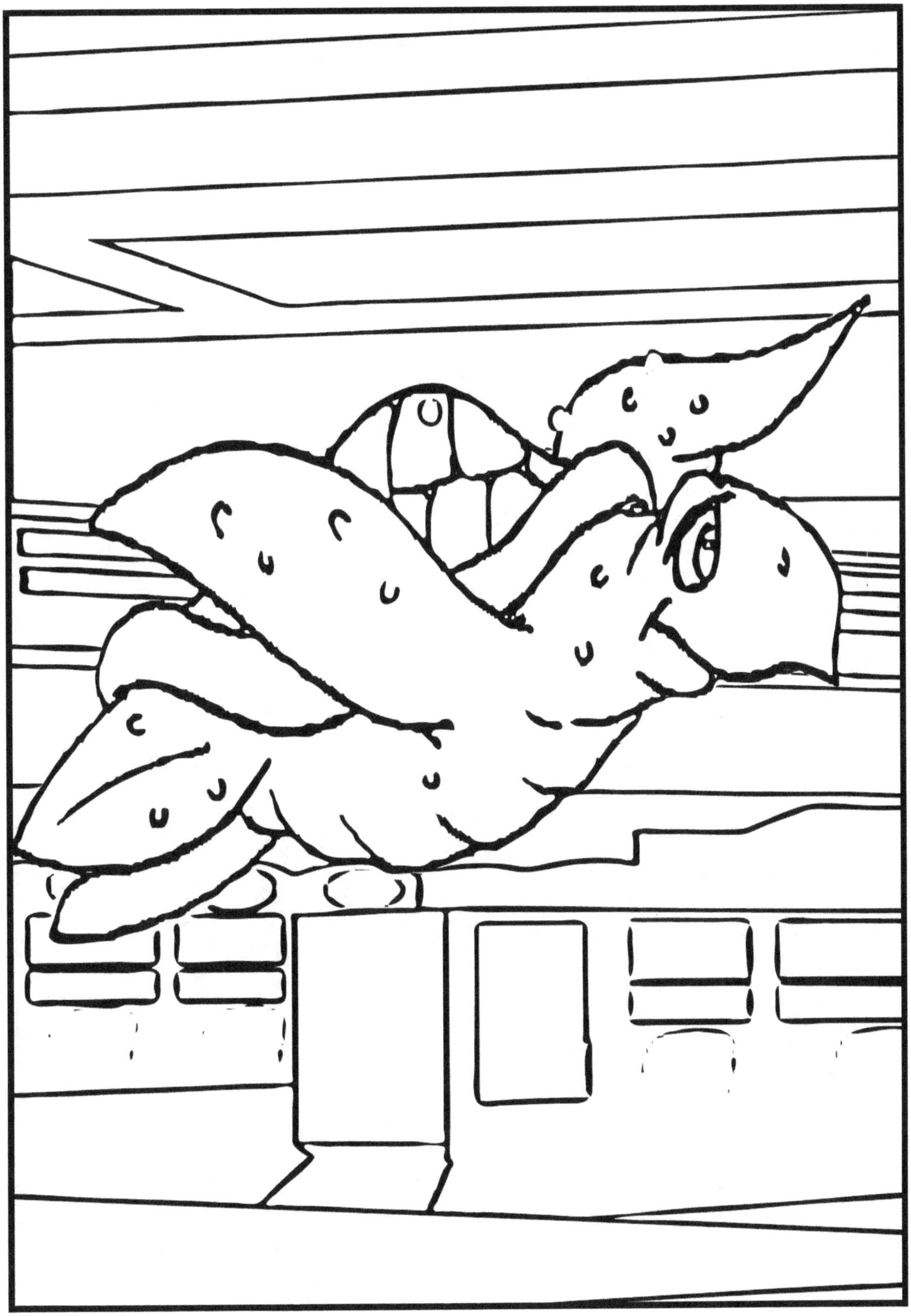

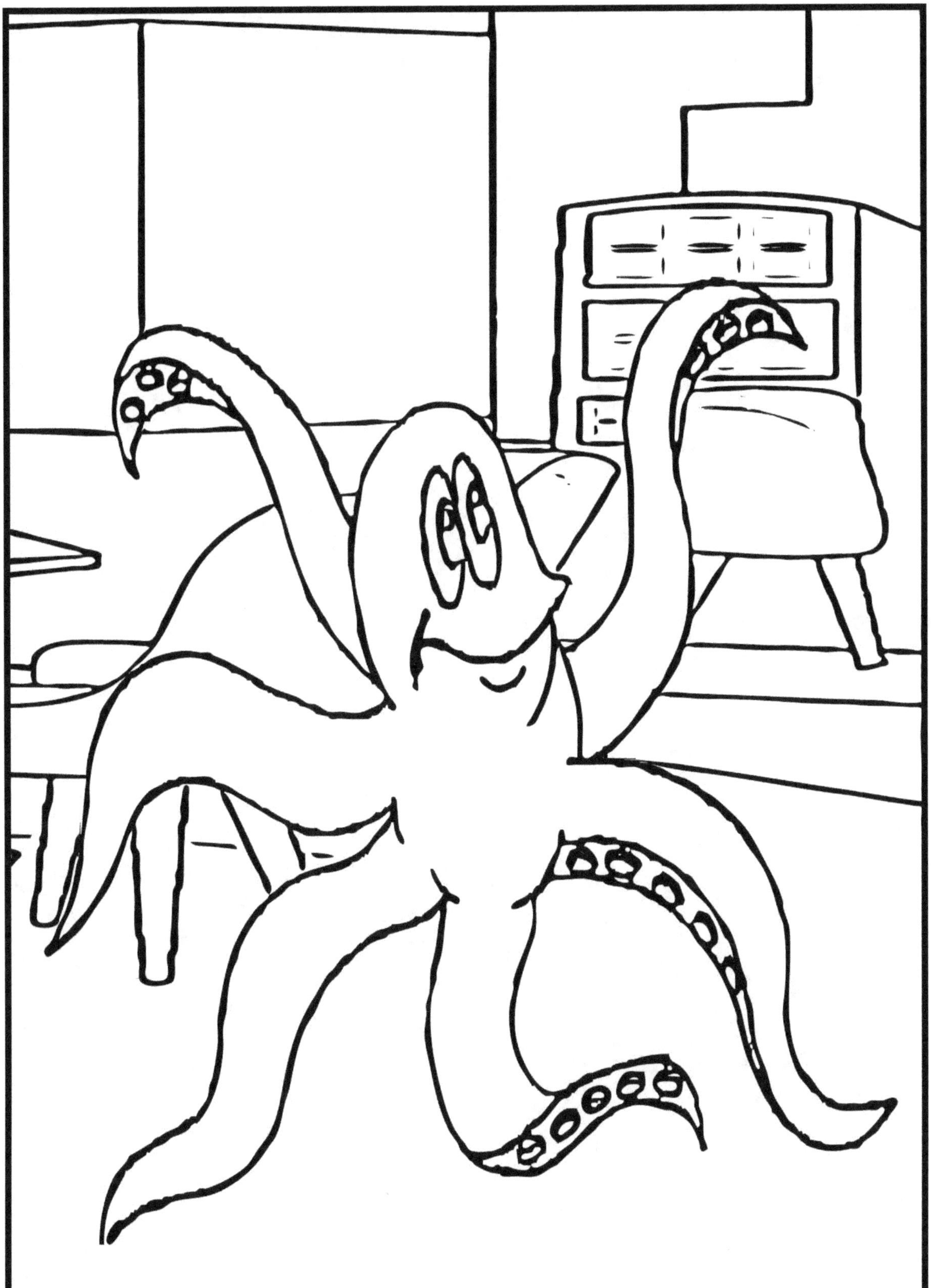

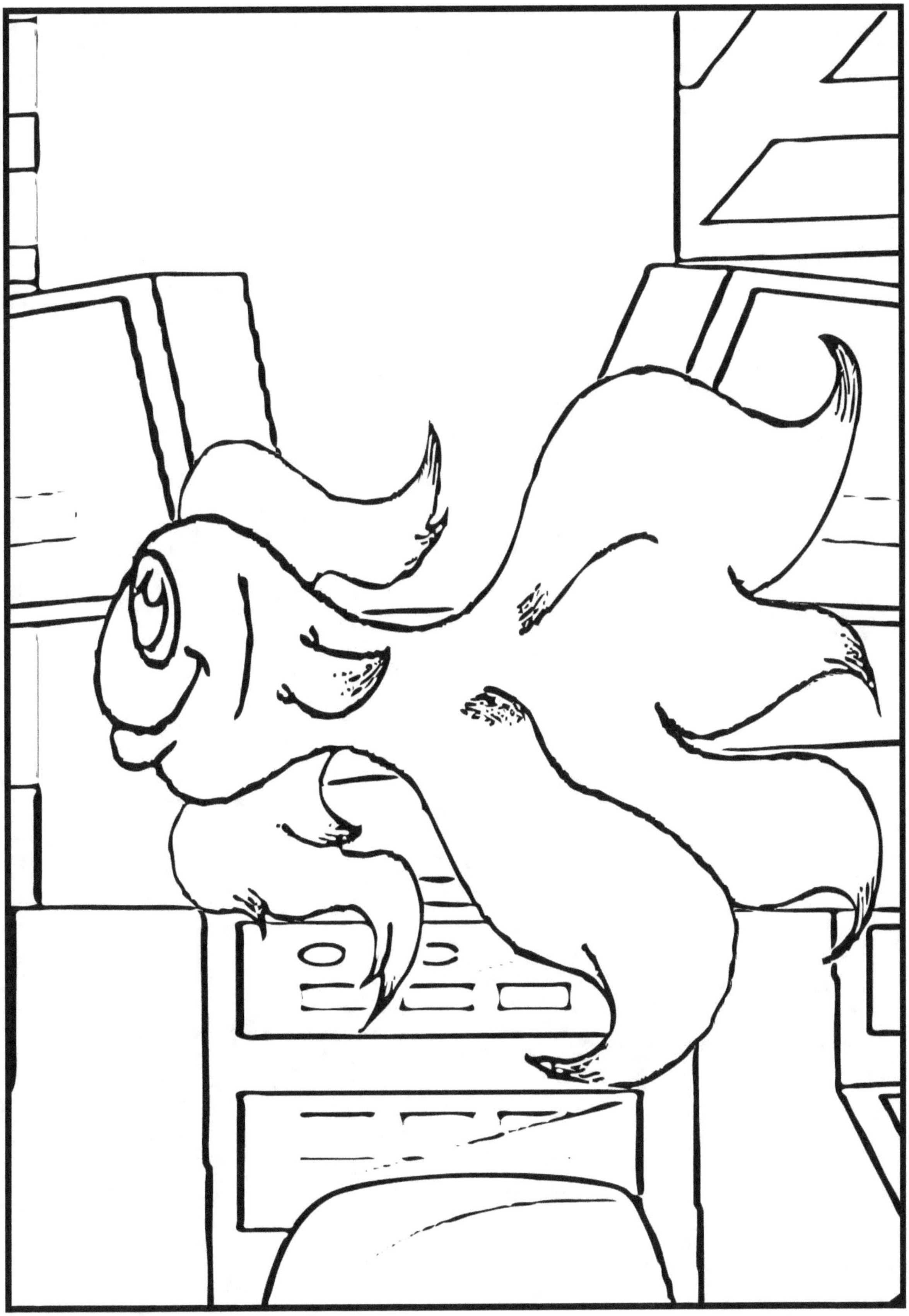

www.ingramcontent.com/pod-product-compliance
Lightning Source LLC
Chambersburg PA
CBHW081311180526
45170CB00007B/2659
* 9 7 8 1 5 2 2 8 8 5 9 7 9 *